Seeds of Fortune

Brenda Parkes
Illustrated by Chi Chung

Rigby
A Harcourt Achieve Imprint

www.Rigby.com
1-800-531-5015

Long ago there lived a very wealthy man. Knowing his days were coming to an end, he called his three sons to his bed.

“My sons,” he said, “I have been careful to save as much money as I spend. My last wish is that you share my wealth. Work, save, and always care for each other.”

When the father died, the two eldest sons ignored their father's wishes. They kept all the land for themselves. Handing only a small bag of money to their brother, Luk Sun, they told him, "Make your own way in the world."

Luk Sun and his wife searched for a new home. They were unable to buy a house with their small bag of money. They had almost given up hope when they found a small hut on some rocky land.

Each day the couple worked very hard. Luk Sun and his wife earned money by doing many different chores for their neighbors. They saved all the money they could.

The two worked long hours to clear rocks from their own land. They hoped to someday grow a crop.

Winter was bitterly cold that year. Snow covered the land and the couple could no longer find work. They used their savings to buy food and firewood.

One night they found an old man outside their home. His torn clothes could not shield him from the icy wind.

"You are welcome to come inside and share our food," they said. "You will not survive the night outside."

The old man stayed until the first signs of spring.

When he left, he gave them three small seeds. “I am grateful for your kindness,” he said. “Plant these tonight and you will have food and shelter for the rest of your days.”

The couple planted the seeds that night.

The next morning the couple was amazed to see green vines covering their land. Within weeks, dozens of golden pumpkins were ready to harvest.

They could hardly believe their good fortune. "We have pumpkins to eat and pumpkins to sell!" cried the wife.

"And seeds to grow another crop," added Luk Sun.

The older brothers planted no crops that spring. They were far too busy enjoying their new riches. They bought the most expensive clothes and jewelry. They ate only the best foods.

Another year went by. Luk Sun and his wife sold two more crops. They bought an ox and cart with the money they earned selling pumpkins. Even so, they saved their money wisely.

During the long winter months, they kept working. They dried pumpkin seeds and made pumpkin flour. Every morning they made a pot of pumpkin soup to share with their neighbors.

Luk Sun's older brothers did no work at all. Weeds grew in their fields. Fruit rotted in their orchards.

"We have more than enough money to last us for the rest of our lives," they bragged. "We never need to work again."

They hired workers to build fine new homes. They filled the houses with the most costly furniture and expensive art.

In the third year, Luk Sun bought more land. He hired helpers and greatly increased the number of pumpkins that he grew. Soon he had saved enough for a new house.

The older brothers faced hard times. They had been careless with their father's money and had run out. They had to trade their fine clothes for food.

The two brothers set out to find work. No one would hire them, so they decided to look in other villages. Many miles and many villages later, they came to Luk Sun's farm.

They greedily began to plan how they could share his fortune. “Dear brother,” they said, “remember our father’s last wish. We have fallen on hard times and need your help.”

“My brothers,” he replied, “I will gladly share my good fortune with you.”

The brothers smiled. They began dreaming of how they would spend the money.

Luk Sun gave each of them a small pouch. “My fortune began with three seeds,” he said. “Work hard and save, and you, too, will have a fortune.”

The brothers were unhappy that Luk Sun did not give them money. They angrily threw down the pouches. They left, never knowing they had tossed away the seeds of a fortune.

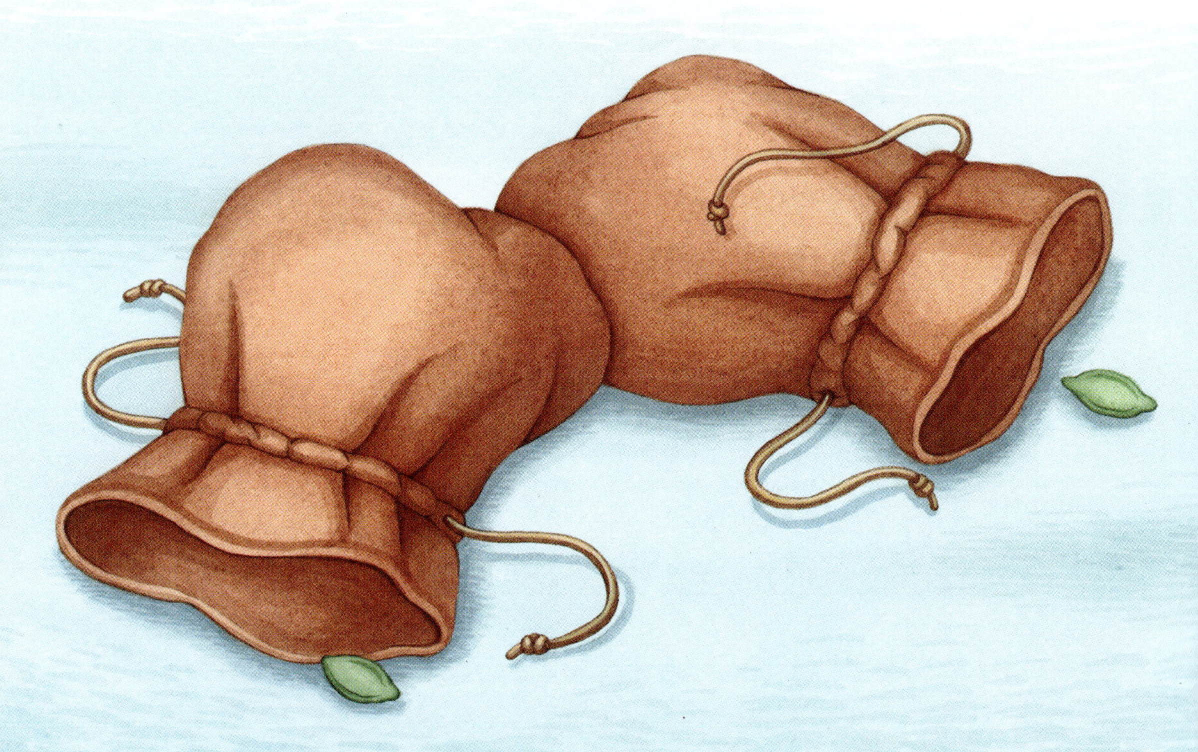